to all the girls who
have had to fight
againts cancer

Hope & Healing © 2022
Written by Liezari Grobler
Illustrations by Frances Tomaselli
Proofread & Edited by Katinka Joubert
All rights reserved.
ISBN: 9798825482668

# content

*liezari grobler*

Hi, my name is Liezari Grobler. My friends and family call me Liellie.
I am a daughter of King Jesus, who is still busy writing His story for my life.
I was born on the 3rd of June 1993 in Pretoria, where I grew up with my dearest
sister, Suzanne, and loving parents, Susan and Kobus. I matriculated from Die
Afrikaanse Hoër Meisieskool Pretoria (2011) and continued to earn my Science
degree in Human Genetics from the University of Pretoria.
My interests changed from year to year, but all for the best because I eventually
found my true gift: teaching!

In 2016 I moved to Kleinmond in the Western Cape, where I worked as an instructor in movement education for Monkeynastix. A year later I moved to Cape Town where I was a teacher for three years at Star College Cape Town. In 2020 I started with a new teaching position in Science, at Curro Uitzicht Independent School, but I recently embarked on a journey to the UK and I am excited to see where God leads me.

Family and friends play a vital part in my life. Even though I lived very isolated for some periods, it was my family and friends who played the most significant role in my journey. Relationally I was challenged, but through it all, I realised the true blessing of family and friendships. God knew exactly what I needed in every season of my life, and He provided. With some friends, God knits our hearts together, and we will stay friends for life, whereby others were just in my life for a season – and I will always be thankful to them.

This book has been written since 2006. Initially, I made it my Project with a Purpose – something had to come from the pain that I have endured. Over the years, I wrote bits and pieces, but I never knew what would become of it.

A few years later, Frances Tomaselli stepped into my life. Since day one, she brought colour to my life. Frances has the softest heart and purest intentions. She lays her life down daily for her loved ones and cares about everyone around her. For some time, we were going through different seasons, but our friendship was rekindled and more profound than ever before. God knew exactly that we needed each other for the seasons to come.

We went through many challenges together. When I was hopeless, Frances was the one who reminded me of God's hope and His healing. We shed many tears and had many outbursts of laugher as we shared our hearts and dreams. And somehow our separate ideas became one... Hope and Healing.

She witnessed the pain that I went through and the testimony that came from it, and she wanted to bring the story to life. So we teamed up together to make this book a reality. Her illustrations are personal and inspired by God because she can also testify of Hope and Healing in her own life. This is a story from our hearts and personal experiences with God to you.

As you read this testimony, my wish for you is to be inspired by the Saving Grace of God and to realise that He is still working in your life. May you be filled with Hope for your future.

we are afraid of losing
what we have, whether it's
our life or our possessions
and property. but this fear
evaporates when we
understand that our life
stories and the history of
the world were written
by the same hand.
— paulo coelho

# CHAPTER 1

# one life, live it

We all see life in a different way. Whether it is "Life is like a box of chocolates" or "Life is like a roller-coaster". We all picture our lives in a certain way. I, however, have a few ideas to describe life and specifically my life. Overall my life experiences led me to believe that life is like a story that you can tell. One of my favourite authors explained it profoundly.

Our life is a story. A rather long and complicated story that has unfolded over time. There are many scenes, large and small, and many "firsts." Your first step, your first word, your first day of school. There was your first best friend, your first recital; your first date; your first love; your first kiss; your first heartbreak. If you stop and think of it, your heart has lived through quite a story thus far. And over the course of that story, your heart has learned many things.    (John Eldredge, Waking The Dead)

Like any other book, my life story consists out of chapters. Now you may ask if there is a chapter for each of my living years or by what means do I identify a chapter in my life. That brings me to the second theme of my life: Seasons. Each chapter in my life story tells of a different season in my life. As you read through my life story, you will see that I faced many challenges, as well as many happy and blessed times. The seasons of my life were not all the same, and they all came to an end for a new season to begin. I can reflect and identify seasons where God taught me different life lessons and carried me through specific situations. Some seasons had themes, whereas in respect of others, I am still trying to figure out why things happened as they did and what I was supposed to learn from them.

Lastly, but most importantly, I must mention that when I surrendered my life to God, I realised that He is in control of my life. That is why I see God as the Author of my life story. God, as Creator, spoke the world into existence. He upholds His Creations by the word of His power. The best of all is that all the days ordained for us were written in a Book before one of them came to be.

He already planned my life when I was in my mother's womb. Please don't misunderstand and think that I am just a puppet that has no choice in life, on the contrary.

Through Jesus Christ, I have the freedom and can live the abundant life He came to give me. He gave me the freedom of choice, but still, I can be sure that every detail of my life of love for God is worked into something good. No one knows me better than He does. Only He knows my heart's deepest desires, and He wants to give me a life that surpasses my biggest expectations and dreams. So I want to live the life He intended for me. I want to live the life that He has authored for me.

The life story which God has written for me (and is still writing), is filled with exciting times. I always knew that my life is like no other and that it testifies about God's greatness and faithfulness. Even when times look dark, He has a way out as well as a way to take me higher than I was before. My greatest desire is to use the life story He has given me to testify about Christ, the Hope of the World.

Therefore, I ultimately see my life as His Story, My Testimony.

behold,
he makes
all things
new

# a story to tell

I have a great passion for listening to the stories of people and learning from them. I love meeting new people and listening to how they've journeyed to where they are. When someone tells you their story, you can relate to parts of their journey. You can be inspired and learn from their successes, or you can listen to their mistakes and make a mental note for your own life.

Someone once said, why do you want to learn from your own mistakes when you can learn from someone else's?

We are all unique and have our own stories to tell. Never underestimate the power of a personal testimony. God has walked you through situations that only you know of. You knew how you felt during the time and what you would have wanted to hear for your own comfort and to help you keep going. Someone else may walk a similar road, and they need your encouragement. No matter how big or small the case, you can always mean something to somebody.

Ten years ago, I started writing my testimony. Each time I got discouraged. Whether it was a lack of words and inspiration, or the enemy trying to hold me back, I just didn't know how to put my story into writing. I didn't know where to begin or in which way I must write it. I felt a stirring in my heart to share with others what God did in my life and is still doing. Something purposeful came out of my difficult times and all was not in vain. I want people to remember me, not as the girl who was sick or by what I did. When they think of me or hear my story, they must be in awe of God's greatness and faithfulness.

When I was 12 years old, I got my first journal. It had a cerise pink cover, and the pages had golden edges. In the beginning I did not know how to use it. I wondered if I had to write to someone or just to myself. Sometime during that year I went through challenging times, and I started writing down my feelings and the events that led to it. It felt so liberating. I expressed some frustrations and thoughts that I struggled with but didn't want to discuss with others. Soon the journal became a tool of reflection, but it also led to the contents of this book.

I wrote about many memorable moments. On the eve of each birthday I wrote about things that happened during the past year which I was thankful for. On the night of my birthday I would write about my wishes for the upcoming year. My journals were filled with love letters about boys and several sad stories about break ups. The pages were filled with my hopes and dreams and also disappointments. I wrote many earnest prayers and cries, seeking God's Voice and His Will. Journalling became a personal time and having conversations with God.

I love to reflect on everything that I wrote. At times it brought abundant laughter and sometimes I was left in awe about how God provided. I then realised that my worries were all for nothing. Reflecting on those moments helped me to take a step back and see everything in view. It gave me another perspective towards hope. And hope is an essential element of growth and healing.

# time to reflect

1.HOW WAS MY LIFE BEFORE I MET JESUS CHRIST
AND ACCEPTED HIM AS MY SAVIOR?

2.HOW DID I COME TO KNOW AND ACCEPT JESUS AS
MY SAVIOR?

3.HOW IS YOUR LIFE SINCE SALVATION, GROWING
IN CHRIST AND SERVING HIM?

"MY MOUTH WILL TELL OF
YOUR RIGHTEOUS ACTS,
OF YOUR DEEDS OF
SALVATION ALL DAY..."
PSALM 71:15

*write your own story*

LIFE BEFORE CHRIST

*"throw off your old sinful nature and your former way of life, which is corrupted by lust and deception."*
*— ephesians 4:22*

No direction
Wrong relationships
Impure
Something missing
Good person
Emptiness
Religious
Without purpose
Good deeds
Lonely
Fear of death
Fearful
Driven
Controlling

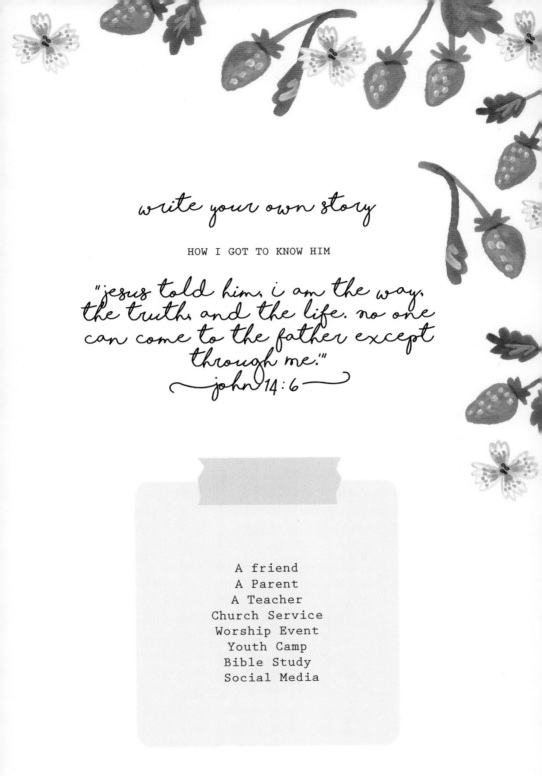

*write your own story*

HOW I GOT TO KNOW HIM

*"jesus told him, i am the way, the truth, and the life. no one can come to the father except through me."*
*john 14:6*

A friend
A Parent
A Teacher
Church Service
Worship Event
Youth Camp
Bible Study
Social Media

*write your own story*

MY CHANGED LIFE

*"now we look inside, and what we see is that anyone united with the messiah gets a fresh start, is created new. the old life is gone; a new life burgeons! look at it!"*
*— 2corinthians 5:17 —*

Joy
Patience
Love
Hope
Contentment
Service
Peace
Kindness
Self-control
Assurance
Sensitivity
Faithfulness
Compassion
Gentleness

YOU
MAKE ALL
THINGS
NEW

# childhood building blocks

When I reflect on the story of my life, I see it as a great adventure. There were more ups than downs. Fortunately I have special memories. I recall many hours at the back of a '110 Land Rover Defender on road trips to my father's next diving adventure – mostly Ponta du Ouro. I was in my happy place when we were camping just meters from the beach. We spent our days building sand castles and swimming from dusk till dawn. This is how I recall my life – around holidays. We were fortunate enough for my father to take us places, even abroad. My childhood life experiences mostly came from the holidays we took. Visually, I can imagine myself going back to those times and even recall the specific music that played in the background.

Apart from the holidays, my childhood is a blur. I vaguely remember the times that I landed myself in hospital and playing with friends. My faith was based on Sunday church services. I believed in God and His existence, but I did not enjoy waking up early on a Sunday morning to go to church. Some days I even pretended to fall asleep again after my mother woke me up, just to use the excuse that I overslept and not be ready for church in time. On the days I attended Kids' Church, I used to make up theories about what I thought the Bible stories taught us – unfortunately it was never in line with what the teacher told us.

Death wasn't a topic I often thought about. Our family and friends were blessed to be well and alive during my childhood and I was never confronted with death or funerals. I knew it was a reality, but it was something I regarded as unimportant. Unfortunately that is how I often deal with hardships in life. If it makes me uncomfortable or I don't understand it or I feel unable to handle it, I just don't think about it.

When I was six years old, my maternal grandmother got cancer.
I didn't know what it was. I just knew that she was sick and that
everyone was concerned about her life. The next time I saw
her she was bald. I then figured out that she had skin cancer.
Unfortunately her cancer was too advanced, and not long after
that she passed away.

That was my first encounter with cancer and death. Those two
were automatically linked in my mind. As a six-year-old, I was in a
crucial stage of development and learning, therefore I concluded
that cancer is a death sentence.

I was once asked on a youth camp to draw a time line of my life.
We didn't have much time, but I quickly drew what stood out as
life events. Afterwards as we reflected on our time lines, I realised
that  the events that I had mentioned were either vacations or
sickness in our family and the deaths of my grandparents.  It
saddens me as I realise that I regarded the smaller events in my
life as insignificant and that is far from what they truly mean to
me. Tough times indeed build our character, but the less dramatic
events also shape our thoughts, dreams, and goals. It is my
constant goal to live more in the moment and cherish the small
things in my day-to-day life.

my life

brainstorm - plot

# timeline

key events - reflect - fill the gaps

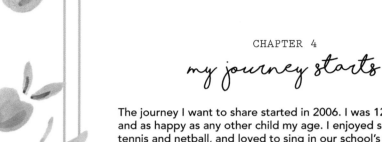

CHAPTER 4

*my journey starts*

The journey I want to share started in 2006. I was 12 years old and as happy as any other child my age. I enjoyed school, played tennis and netball, and loved to sing in our school's Christian performing group. I had a fantastic group of friends and I was excited to be in the last year of primary school.

I was so busy with school activities that I didn't pay much attention to the recurrent symptoms I was experiencing. I thought that my extreme tiredness was due to my busy schedule. It went on for far too long. Eventually, we thought it best to go for further testing. Initially, we suspected that it might be diabetes as the tiredness could be seen as low blood sugar. We had a family history of diabetes.

I remember that day crystal clear. On Wednesday, 15 March 2006, we had an appointment for blood tests. They tested for everything. I drank the glucose solution for the diabetes test. I recall that I felt terrible afterwards and was therefore convinced that it was diabetes.

After the blood tests, I went back to school, but I was not well. I had netball practice after school, and I didn't know where I would get the energy to warm-up and do all the exercises. When I went to change one of my friends came to me and told me that my mother was there for me. Her expression immediately told me that something was wrong. I was concerned that something had happened to my father or sister, but she assured me that they were all right. I then realised it must have had something to do with the results of the blood tests.

My mother said that the doctor wanted to consult with us as soon as possible. My father even had to come from a business trip out of town to attend the appointment. I immediately figured that this was no regular doctor's appointment.

We drove to The Little Company of Mary's Oncology Centre, as it was known back then, where we were met with Doctor Lourens de Jager. My head was spinning with thoughts about my fate.

That afternoon I was diagnosed with Acute Lymphoblastic Leukemia (ALL). ALL is a type of blood cancer that develops from white blood cells – the cells that form our immunity - in the bone marrow. Our bone marrow is the soft inner part of our bones that produces all our stem cells. Stems cells need to differentiate into different blood cells (white blood cells, red blood cells and blood platelets) that serve a vital role in our bodies. My stem cells that had to differentiate into white blood cells changed into cancerous cells.

My first reaction to the shocking news was one of total disbelief. I thought it couldn't be possible because I was not bald. My only reference to cancer was of the melanoma that my grandmother had. Her hair fell out because she had cancer. I am not even bald, how is it possible that I could have cancer? I was under the wrong impression that that hair loss was a symptom of cancer and not a side effect of the treatment for the disease. The doctor calmly explained that my hair would fall out once I began with chemotherapy.

For the rest of the meeting, we talked about the road ahead. The doctor explained the treatment plan and what I could expect, but I couldn't give it much attention. I only had one question looming in my mind: "Am I going to die?"

Cancer and death have long since been linked in my mind. I didn't know about any cure or treatment at that time. I just remembered how quickly my grandmother died after I heard that she had cancer.

We drove home in silence that afternoon. We were drained from shock. It felt like the carpet was just abruptly pulled out from under my feet. There were outbursts of tears and questioning thoughts because we didn't know what the future held. The hardest part lay ahead - to share the news with my close friends and family.

When we told my sister her reaction was unexpected. She was furious with us because she thought we were joking with her. She was in disbelief and it broke my heart all over again to see how saddened she was by the news. At that moment, I realised the enormity of the situation. It was about to change, not only my life, but also the life of those close to me.

That evening I couldn't sleep. The fear of the unknown got so overwhelming that I got up, took my duvet and pillow, and went to lie down on the floor next to my mother's bed. I realised she was not sleeping either, and we held hands for the rest of the evening.

The next day I was booked for surgery and to start with chemotherapy. We also visited my primary school to share the news and to arrange for the practicalities regarding my absence from school. It was my last year of primary school, and I was concerned about my academics and the challenges that I had to face to keep up with my work. The school was very supportive. All my friends and teachers expressed their condolences and wished me all the best for the journey ahead.

It was difficult to see them and go through all the emotions again. Facts became reality and I realised how much I would be missing. But God knows our needs...

When one of the teachers walked passed me in the school's corridor, he, with tears in his eyes, gave me a piece of paper. I will never forget his message because it immediately gave me peace of mind about the future. I held on to it ever since. The note with scripture made an impression on me for the rest of my life:

Lizari
Jer. 29:11 (Lees)
Ek dink aan jou
en bid vir jou!
Mnr. Rudolph

**DANKIE RUDOLPH**

Jeremiah 29:11 (Read)
I'm thinking of you and praying for you.
Mr. Rudolph

We didn't waste time. After the school visit, we drove directly to the hospital. I was booked for the port-a-cath insertion and chemotherapy after that. The port-a-cath is a port that is attached to a catheter which is inserted into a large vein in your chest. They use it for the treatment. On my way to the theatre there was a delay. Whilst waiting to be pushed in the nurses tried to make small talk. One of the nurses was combing her fingers through my hair and out of the blue said, "It's such a pity that your beautiful hair would need to be shaved off." That hit me hard. It was the first time that I realised that I was going to lose my hair. It was such a shock and since I was so sensitive at the time, I realised that I would have to make peace with it.

→»··«←

My life came to a complete stand still after I was diagnosed, or that was how it felt. I realised that I had to leave everything I was busy with and first deal with cancer. I couldn't attend school or take part in any of my other activities. I needed to receive intense chemotherapy, and due to the effect that it had on my immune system, I had to isolate myself. No public places or contact with limited people. For a 12 year old that was a harsh sentence.

My treatment was aggressive. It consisted of many phases that ranged between different intensities of chemotherapy and radiation. Sometimes I received chemo while being hospitalised. On other occasions it was a daily treatment. At times I would also have had to go three times a week and be there for the whole day. Either my mother, sister, or father would go with me and they were the best support system any patient could ever ask for.

I mostly had positive thoughts. Although I realised that death was a possibility I focused on recovering and continuing with my healthy life. I had faith and often prayed that God would protect me and heal me from cancer. I was so grateful for the support I had. Many family members and friends prayed for me and visited me. I can never thank them enough for standing by me during those times.

I spent my days in and out of the hospital for tests and treatment. I regularly underwent a lumbar puncture where they insert a needle into the lower part of the spine to collect cerebrospinal fluid and also administer chemo.

After each phase of treatment a bone marrow biopsy was done to extract bone marrow and to determine how I was responding to the treatment. Fortunately, the treatment was a success, and I was in complete remission after only four months.
That means that the tests and physical examinations showed that all signs of the leukemia were gone. I, however, needed to complete all the remaining phases of the treatment to prevent any relapse of the disease.

I truly believe that God was my Provider and my Healer. It was He who protected me through it all and healed me. There were many risks during my treatment, but I stayed healthy and reacted well towards the treatment. I experienced a real-life miracle from God, healing me from cancer.

→»··«←

My blood counts were almost back to normal, and I could return to school. Slowly but surely my life returned to normal. I was motivated to make the best of every moment and even catch up on all that I had lost. I finished primary school and got promoted to high school.

The prospect of high school was daunting. Like any other eight-grader, I was scared about the BIG school and the BIG matrics. I had to face another challenge though because I had little confidence. It felt like I stood out like a sore thumb. I had gained a lot of weight due to the cortisone that I had to take as part of my treatment. I was also still bald and had to wear a hat to school. I felt insecure because I attracted attention wherever I went.

I felt sensitive and self conscious because the other learners were curious about my situation. I remember how I would walk in the corridors when a boy would grab the hat off my head. Those were embarrassing moments, but luckily I became used to it and gained confidence again. I knew it would only be a short while before my hair would grow back. I realised that I could use those vulnerable moments as opportunities to share my story and testify about what God did in my life.

Eventually my life resumed to normal. At the start of grade ten, I transferred to another school with more opportunities. I embraced life, thankful that God healed me from my cancer. I was still on maintenance treatment, where I went for monthly check-ups and received small dosages of chemo. I didn't dread it because each month, I was reminded of God's grace in the past. It motivated me to trust Him in every situation that lay ahead. When they removed my port-o-catheter in 2009 it gave me a sense of finality. Whilst it remained in me, there was always a chance that they might still need to use it. But when it was removed, I felt that I got closure after the whole process.

Even though I told myself that the cancer was something of the past it still lingered. I would often be reminded of what I went through and it would trigger those memories. It wasn't always bad. I had learned a lot of life's lessons which I would never forget. That season of difficulty shaped me and I therefore didn't mind being reminded about it.

The thing about cancer is that it steals time, opportunities, and often your self-worth or identity. My life during that season was mostly about me. You see, the fact that I was vulnerable to infections caused the need for our family's lifestyle to be adapted. Everything was arranged around my needs and specifications. My family needed to compromise and put me first. Many of my parents' and my sister's friends couldn't come to visit because they were sick and posed a risk to me. My parents had to take me for treatment and had to attend to my needs all the time. The result was that my sister often had to take second best. Do you pick up where the focus was? It was all on me. It was the season of me, myself and I. I tried my best, and my family supported me in the best way they could. Unfortunately it cultured a lot of self-centredness.

I was so used to things going my way and the attention I got from all the support that I had a tough time adapting when it all returned to normal. I reached a point after my journey with cancer when I realised that I was too self-centred and caught up in my own life that I forgot to look up to Him. I was disappointed and unhappy about the time that I had lost as a result of my illness. I therefore didn't realise what it taught me and what I gained during that season.

This is when the journaling became very valuable again. I read my past entries and reflected on the challenges and victories. I will never forget that one day when I was worshipping and praying to God, the enormity of His work in my life suddenly dawned on me. The most remarkable thing that was revealed to me was that even when I didn't have the greatest faith, didn't feel so close to God or prayed so often, He was still there for me. He was constant no matter how near or far I felt from Him. I realised that when I was weak and sick the prayers of those around me were heard and answered! That left me in complete awe and thankfulness.

I had to go through a season where I repented about my self-centredness and mindfully put those around me first. It is an ongoing process. I have to lay myself down every day and use every opportunity I get to share my testimony with others making Him the centre of it all and honouring those who supported and prayed for me.

CHAPTER 5

# wholeheartedly

"And whatever you do, do
it heartily, as to the
Lord and not to men"
Colossians 3:23 (NKJV)

For the first time, as I was moving into a new season, I could look ahead. My hope for the future was to wholeheartedly commit to a dream, and specifically a dream that aligns with God's will and purpose for my life.

But ever since I was a little girl I experienced many disappointments. Whether it was a toy that I desperately wanted or a holiday I wished for. Often things didn't turn out the way I wanted them to. It soon became clear to me that it is too heartbreaking to desperately wish or hope for something and then learn that it will not materialise. Eventually, I tried to protect myself from these disappointments by not getting my hopes up too high. I automatically tried to protect myself in the same way with the dreams that I had for my future. I didn't want to dream too big because the disappointments will be too great if it didn't materialise.

Time and again we put our hearts wholeheartedly on things that are tangible and fleeting. Those things, however, often disappoint us and make us sad. God has other plans for our everyday life and also for our future. We can put our trust in Him wholeheartedly when we dream and hope for anything that aligns with His will.

"above all else,
guard your heart,
for it is the
wellspring of life."
proverbs 4:23

# you are captivating

Above all else. Why?
Because God knows that our heart is core to who we are. It is the true source of all creativity, courage, and conviction. It is the fountainhead of our faith, our hope, and of course, our love. This "wellspring of life" within us is the very essence of our existence, the centre of our being.

Your heart as a woman is the most important thing about you. God loves you – more than you yet know or believe.

Your heart matters to Him!

God did not place these longings in our hearts to torment us. Instead, they reveal the secret of who we truly are and the role that is ours to play. There is so much hope here, hope to become the woman you secretly long to be, the woman who is romanced, irreplaceable, and utterly beautiful.

*This section is made up out of parts taken from the book, Captivating, by John and Stasi Eldredge*

# wonderfully made
## bread + wine

Your thoughts for me, how vast they are
Outnumber sands, upon the shore
I can't attain; how deep You love me

You hemmed me in, behind before
You laid your hand, upon me Lord
I can't attain; how deep You love me

'cause I am fearfully and wonderfully made
Oh I am fearfully and wonderfully made
Oh I am fearfully and wonderfully made
To bring You praise

From dust to gold, You fashioned me
You saw my days, my destiny
I can't attain, your vision for me

And oh I am fearfully and wonderfully made
Oh I am fearfully and wonderfully made
Oh I am fearfully and wonderfully made
To bring You praise

Filled with your glory
Filled with your Spirit
Made in our majesty

Born to bring You praise
And oh I am fearfully and wonderfully made
To bring You praise

What does the word hope mean to you?
Is it something futile – just a wish - or is it something you
have the assurance to realise. Hope is something that shows
potential, stirs up excitement and causes people to take
risks. It is also something that can break hearts, shatter
dreams and make you feel hopelessly defeated.

The Bible speaks a great deal about hope. In Hebrews 11:1
(TPT), we read that "faith brings our hopes into reality and
becomes the foundation needed to acquire the things we
long for." Faith is the key to turn the unseen (hopes) into the
seen (reality).

Are you hoping to find a husband, or for a promotion at
work? Do you have high hopes to reach an exercise goal,
or are you hoping for a friend that will stand by your side.
No matter what you are hoping for, as long as it aligns with
God's will, faith is the key to bring those hopes into reality.

CHAPTER 6

*in the prime of my life*

Talking about hope for a bright future. I had high expectations for my future. My experience as a patient in and out of hospital, made me realise that I have a great interest in biological sciences and specifically in medicine. I was thankful for every doctor who treated me that I decided that I wanted to become a Paediatrician to offer someone else the same hope that they provided to me. I figured that my childhood experience as a cancer patient would make me a good and empathetic doctor. This made me goal-driven and ambitious about my future.

I kept this dream alive for the duration of high school. I enjoyed academics and worked hard to achieve good marks and be accepted at university to study medicine. I didn't just focus on academics. I enjoyed playing tennis and our team played tournaments at schools in other provinces too. I was fortunate enough to be a part of the school's choir. We sang across the country and participated in a competition in Prague. Above it all - I had the best friends to share every moment with.

I was blessed with a healthy, full life, and was content. I saw the oncologist for yearly check-ups. All was well and I was in the prime of my youth.

When I reached my matric year in 2011 I was more determined than ever to finish school on a high note and pursue my dream of becoming a doctor.

The year started with great excitement. I was fortunate enough to be one of the leaders and we orientated the new grade eights. Our program was filled with activities. I was also training for the tennis season and rehearsing for the choir. Schoolwork was escalating and we were continuously reminded about how important good marks were for being accepted into the university program of our choice. There was a buzz at school as all the matrics were talking about their hopes and dreams for the future. It was daunting to think about the big decisions that had to be made but also an exciting time filled with potential and possibilities.

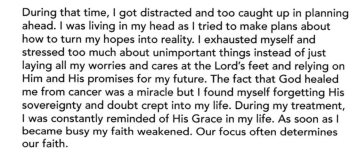

During that time, I got distracted and too caught up in planning ahead. I was living in my head as I tried to make plans about how to turn my hopes into reality. I exhausted myself and stressed too much about unimportant things instead of just laying all my worries and cares at the Lord's feet and relying on Him and His promises for my future. The fact that God healed me from cancer was a miracle but I found myself forgetting His sovereignty and doubt crept into my life. During my treatment, I was constantly reminded of His Grace in my life. As soon as I became busy my faith weakened. Our focus often determines our faith.

"THE DESERT AND THE
PERCHED LAND WILL BE GLAD,
THE WILDERNESS WILL REJOICE
AND BLOSSOM."

isaiah 35:1

CHAPTER 7

## my call to be brave

During March of that year I went for my annual check-up to the doctor. He was so proud and happy to see how healthy I was. That fuelled me to work harder and chase the dream.

Later that month, we went on a tennis tour to Cradock. We had to fly there, and it just added to the fun. Our team was great and the school that hosted the tournament planned so many fun activities apart from the exciting matches that we played. We had the time of our lives and came back with many memories. Unfortunately, that was not all that I came back with.

I had flu symptoms that kept recurring. Even after a few cycles of antibiotics I didn't recover. After the trip, I went to my general practitioner for examination. He saw spots on my legs and suggested blood tests for tick fever. I was unusually tired, but I thought it was just the strain of the tennis and catching up with schoolwork.

I used the sick leave to my benefit to work on a big accounting project that was due in a few weeks. I was focused and wanted to do well.

During that time my father walked into my room. I was a bit agitated because I wanted to get things done before I went back to school. I felt he was interrupting me. When he sat on my bed, and I saw the expression on his face I realised that he wasn't there for a casual conversation. He had bad news from the doctor. It was not good: I had a relapse from my leukemia.

The results from my blood tests showed that the cancerous cells had returned. I was stunned! It hit me out of the blue.

Once again my world came to a complete stand still. I put down my pen and stopped what I was doing. The realisation dawned on me: I was not going to finish that project. I was not going to feel better soon. I was not going to school again. I needed to halt, be brave to face cancer again, and fight for my life.

It was only a month since my previous check up! Questions kept on tormenting me. What could have happened so quickly in a month's time? Did the doctor miss it? Do I need to get treatment again? Am I going to lose my hair? What did I do to make it come back? Did I stress too much? Will I be able to be healed again? What about school? What about matric? What about my dream?

The questions were overwhelming. The uncertainty frightening!

The only thing I knew at that moment was the fact that it was going to be a BIG battle to fight.

"lovely one,
if you dare to dream,
you must be brave
enough to fight!"
girls with swords,
lisa bevere

CHAPTER 8

## the battle we fight

I had another battle to fight against cancer. As daughters of God, we are all in a constant battle. We fight as warrior women in the good fight for our lives. Due to our inheritance as godly royalty, we are warrior princesses of God who must stand our ground in the battle that God has already delivered us from. Even when our future looks unknown, we must rest our hope and faith in Him.

"For You have armed me with strength for the battle."
Psalm 18:39

We are equipped to overcome our challenges. God gave us The Armour to wear and protect us from any arrows that the enemy may fire at us. I knew that I would go through hell but I had to keep going. I believed that God wouldn't allow the relapse to happen if I wasn't strong enough to fight the battle. I couldn't set up camp in hell because I had a journey ahead and I had to see how God would deliver me. One of my favourite Scriptures is 2 Chronicles 17:20 (NLT):

"But you will not even need to fight. Take your positions; then stand still and watch the Lord's victory. He is with you, O people of Judah and Jerusalem. Do not be afraid or discouraged. Go out against them tomorrow, for the Lord is with you!"

Just as hard labour precedes natural birth, so there are temporal battles before eternal dreams. Hard times often indicate the start of a breakthrough of something new and significant. I had to stand my ground and see how He will deliver me.

We all have personal battles that we need to fight. No battle is too big or too small to bring before God. He has given us all we need to fight. We just need to gather all our strength and courage and put on the Full Armour of God. Then we will have victory over all hell on earth.

*This section is made up out of parts taken from the book, Girls With Swords, by Lisa Bevere*

"YOU WILL SHOW ME THE
PATH OF LIFE;
IN YOUR PRESENCE IS
FULLNESS OF JOY;
AT YOUR RIGHT HAND ARE
PLEASURES FOREVERMORE."
PSALM 16:11

# my feet were failing

It felt surreal. There I was, back in Doctor de Jager's rooms, just like five years ago, discussing my battle plan to fight the disease again. Unfortunately, each time cancer relapses, it is more aggressive since the cancer cells become resistant to the previous treatment. Luckily in my case the cancer was detected early but the prognosis was still severe. The doctor explained that we would need to consider a bone marrow transplant to prevent another relapse.

As previously mentioned your bone marrow is the source of all cells in your body. It produces stem cells that differentiate into different cells. My bone marrow produced cancerous blood cells. Having a transplant would replace the faulty source with new healthy cell-producing bone marrow.

However, this procedure was still relatively new and risky at that time. You had to be strong enough to endure the process for it to be a success. The transplant causes your body's immune system to be completely broken down and then be built up from scratch, cell for cell.

We decided to start with chemotherapy immediately before a final decision on the option of a bone marrow transplant was made.

After our visit to the doctor we went to my school to share the news with my friends and discuss the practicalities with the principal. It was hard to tell them and see the shock on their faces. There were many tears but their hugs comforted me and assured me that I wouldn't embark on this journey alone.

The days that followed were filled with visits from people to show their support. I was overwhelmed with gifts, cards and messages from all over. Friends and family surrounded me with their positivity and encouragement. Deep down, however, I was scared. It felt like I was called to walk on water and trust that God will heal me again, but honestly, my faith was weak and my feet were failing. I started doubting and fear crept into my heart. It felt daunting as if I didn't have the "child-like faith" that I once had when I was 12-years old. Why was it so hard to believe a second time? Why did it feel like I was drowning as my feet in faith were failing me?

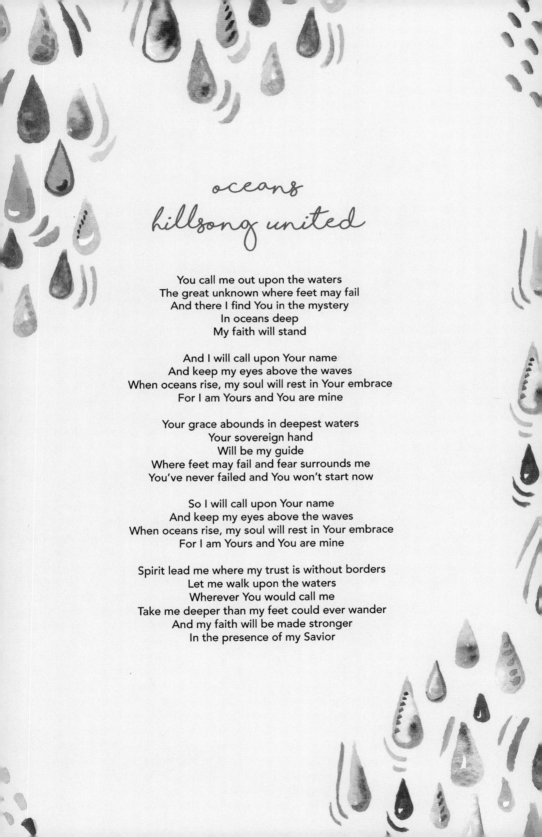

# oceans
# hillsong united

You call me out upon the waters
The great unknown where feet may fail
And there I find You in the mystery
In oceans deep
My faith will stand

And I will call upon Your name
And keep my eyes above the waves
When oceans rise, my soul will rest in Your embrace
For I am Yours and You are mine

Your grace abounds in deepest waters
Your sovereign hand
Will be my guide
Where feet may fail and fear surrounds me
You've never failed and You won't start now

So I will call upon Your name
And keep my eyes above the waves
When oceans rise, my soul will rest in Your embrace
For I am Yours and You are mine

Spirit lead me where my trust is without borders
Let me walk upon the waters
Wherever You would call me
Take me deeper than my feet could ever wander
And my faith will be made stronger
In the presence of my Savior

# the path in life

I sometimes imagine my life like walking on water. There is no path, but for every next step God provides a stone to take the step. Even though I only realised it later, it was precisely where I found myself when I had a relapse.

"Uphold my steps in Your paths,
That my footsteps may not slip."
PSALM 17:5

"You will show me the path of life;
In Your presence is fullness of joy;
At Your right hand are pleasures
forevermore."
PSALM 16:11 (NKJV)

I didn't know where or how I was going to take my next step in the unknown waters, but God was providing for every step along the way.God gives just enough light for the next step in life.It is like stepping stones on a river: They appear once you leap for the next step.

You enlarge my path under me
So my feet did not slip.
PSALM 18:36 (NKJV)

Trust Him with all your heart
Lean not on your own understanding
Acknowledge Him in all you do
And He will direct your path.
PROVERBS 3:5-6 (NKJV)

# you make me brave
## bethel

I stand before You now
The greatness of your renown
I have heard of the majesty and wonder of you
King of Heaven, in humility, I bow

As Your love, in wave after wave
Crashes over me, crashes over me
For You are for us
You are not against us
Champion of Heaven
You made a way for all to enter in

I have heard You calling my name
I have heard the song of love that You sing
So I will let You draw me out beyond the shore
Into Your grace
Your grace

You make me brave
You call me out beyond
the shore into the waves

You make me brave
No fear can hinder now the promises you made

*brave warrior*

Through Jesus Christ we can be
Brave Warriors

- His loves make me brave
- His presence makes me brave
- His faithfulness makes me brave
- His calling makes me brave
- His belief in me makes me brave
- His grace makes me brave

Knowing that God is in control makes me brave!

# diving in

There was no time to waste I had to put on my brave face and dive right into the water. Healing was on the other side and I couldn't give up. Another port-o-cath was inserted through which I received chemotherapy. The initial phase of the treatment was severe. The cancer cells had to be prevented from spreading.

Cancer cells are very resistant. That is why the chemotherapy needed to be so potent. The treatment not only killed the cancer cells, but also destroyed most of my healthy cells. I was exhausted after each treatment and too weak to do anything. Sometimes I couldn't even take a bath on my own and had to be helped by my loving mother and sister. They were always so patient and caring! The treatment also weakened my immune system to such a degree that I couldn't be exposed to any bacteria. I had my 18th birthday during that time but could only celebrate it with a few people due to my low immunity. I kept up with my school work whenever I felt strong enough because I still wanted to finish my matric year. The hopes and dreams in my heart were still strong but I had no idea how the rest of the year would unfold.

After a few months things got better. I responded well to the treatment and the doctor gave us the good news that I was in remission. We were thankful and relieved, but the fight was far from over. We realised that the best way to fight and end this once and for all would be to go ahead with the bone marrow transplant.

We immediately started with the planning and process for it. My sister was tested as a donor but unfortunately she wasn't a match. The next step was to find a donor on the bone marrow registry both nationally and internationally. The doctor suggested that we consider doing the transplant in Cape Town as they had an outstanding medical team and transplant unit. My parents considered the possibilities of the transplant being done in Cape Town. It was a foreign concept to us, and we had concerns about finding the most suitable donor to prevent the risk of my body rejecting the transplant. There were still statistics of unsuccessful transplants that made it hard for us to go through with the process.

The future was unclear and we still had many decisions to make. The transplant sounded drastic and dangerous. We gathered all possible information, but it didn't make the idea of the transplant any easier. We were still searching for a matching donor...

*when facing an unknown situation, where do you put your trust?*

# CHAPTER 11

# deep dark water

Time was of the essence and the risks were high. An infection is a great risk to blood cancer. Due to the low blood counts caused by the chemo a leukemia patient can't afford to be infected. In dire cases it can be fatal since your body will not be able to fight the infection. That is what happened in my case. I reached the deep dark waters.

At the end of July 2011 I got an infection. It started with extreme tiredness, but then the high temperature made us realise that we were dealing with a serious situation. I was immediately admitted to hospital. The infection was so serious that I could not be treated with regular antibiotics and I was transferred to the Intensive Care Unit (ICU).

The infection spread throughout my body and caused multiple life threatening side effects. I had to be sedated to help my body fight the infection. That meant that I was intubated and a feeding tube was inserted - it was all very traumatic. My internist and oncologist tried to identify the type of infection in order to treat it accordingly. Unfortunately it was complicated. The time delay caused that I got weaker and weaker. The tests showed that my heart was fragile due to all the chemotherapy that I had received in the past. I also had Acute Respiratory Distress Syndrome (ARDS) whereby the fluid built up in my lungs and deprived my other organs of the required oxygen to function. My prognosis was bad and my parents were told that I might not make it through the night.

Through God's Grace I made it! I was treated with the right medication and I regained strength and fought the infection. I had no feeling or movement in my body and had to relearn to walk and gain my sensations again. I was discharged after 4 weeks in ICU and one week in the general ward. I was still weak and received regular neurophysiotherapy, but I was healed from the infection.

The neurophysiotherapist was very supportive and she decided that we needed a goal to keep me motivated during the therapy. Our goal was that I had to be healthy and strong enough to attend my matric farewell. Initially I was quite dispirited and didn't want to get my hopes up and be disappointed.

Then one of my close friends visited me in hospital and asked me to be his date to their matric farewell. I was in an all girls school and that was the motivation I needed to attend my farewell too. I then asked him to be my date as well. Their support and belief in me made the world of difference to my recovery.

And so it happened. I recovered in time to attend both matric farewells. We had a great time. I wasn't strong enough to dance, but the time spent with friends was a blessing and we made beautiful memories that I will cherish for the rest of my life. Later in the evening at my friend's matric farewell I started to feel cold. I thought it was normal at first, but then I began to shiver intensely. I called my dad to come and fetch me. It turned out I had another infection and this time it was in my port-o-catheter which was removed immediately to prevent any spread of the infection.

We couldn't proceed with the bone marrow transplant at that time because I was too weak and would not be able to withstand it. I, however, felt good. I was in remission, and I was getting better and stronger every day.

Unfortunately, I could not write my final matric exam because I was too far behind with my schoolwork. I was in a bad emotional state. I didn't want to repeat the year. I was unhappy because all my friends moved on to a new season in their lives. I felt that I was wasting my life. Fortunately, I had the opportunity to write the supplementary exam in March of the following year. It was therefore not necessary repeat the year. I was still miserable and did not know what I would do for the rest of the year. I never planned a gap year. It interfered with my future dreams and plans to study medicine.

For the first time, I was angry – really angry. I started to ask questions such as "Why did it happen to me?" and "What did I do to deserve this?" I was agitated and frustrated with my circumstances. Things didn't turn out as I have planned and I was sidetracked. I felt completely out of control. That is precisely where God wanted me to be. I had to be out of control to realise that He is always in control. He knew what I needed in order to heal physically and emotionally. Even though I had no plan or idea of what the future held, He knew. He was guiding me. He was my Light when I felt overwhelmed by darkness in the deep dark waters and that gave me Hope.

"FOR YOU WILL
LIGHT MY LAMP;
THE LORD MY GOD
WILL ENLIGHTEN
MY DARKNESS."
PSALM 18:28(NKJV)

# follow the lighthouse

God is our Light in the darkness. He will direct us to where we need go, no matter how dark it gets. Unfortunately that isn't always easy. It never is. It requires patience and a double dosage of trust. We need to trust and walk by faith.

For we walk by faith, not by sight.
2 Corinthians 5:7 (NKJV)

God is our Lighthouse and His Word will always lead us to safety. We have to keep faith in situations that seem hopeless and believe until we see breakthroughs happening in our lives.

For You will light my lamp;
The Lord my God will enlighten my darkness.
Psalm 18:28 (NKJV)

I believe that our faith is based on Hope. Based on God's Word, its victory is secured. His Word must shape, mould and frame the image of Hope within us to boldly and effectively confess our faith. Seek His will with all your heart. Stay hungry for His Word – read and meditate on it continuously. It will bring light even in the darkest of days.

Your word is a lamp to guide my feet
and a light for my path.
Psalm 119:105 (NKJV)

# seek and you shall find

The gap year turned out better than I expected. God had a purpose with it. I was able to work through a few things and I learned a lot about myself. I didn't have anything planned for the year. However, many opportunities came my way for which I am still thankful today. It unfolded as time went by and exceeded my expectations!

My tennis coach offered me the opportunity to work for their tennis academy at a few primary schools in Pretoria. I worked with children of different ages. As a result of this experience I realised that I have a passion for children. I enjoyed working with them. I also read and enriched myself spiritually and intellectually with inspirational books. I did things that I never would have had time for. The year improved when my friend, who had moved to New Zealand, invited me to visit him at the end of the year. I wanted to save for my trip so it motivated me to get creative. I had enough time and enjoyed making things with my hands. I plated bracelets and sold them to friends and family. I even joined our church's choir and took some ballroom classes – it was so much fun!

Unfortunately, one of my friends from school also got diagnosed with cancer. We only met again after his treatment, but he was in the same situation that I was – he was forced to take a gap year. He loved to fly-fish, and I also knew a thing or two about fly-fishing, so we made a few fishing trips to retreat and just be in nature.

The year taught me many lessons. I could see that God had a plan and purpose for every opportunity and person that came my way. I saw God at work within me and in those around me.

I had the privilege to witness God's sovereign Will and His perfect timing in my fly-fishing friend's life. This story is so compelling and whenever I think about it, it gives me hope when I feel that things are not going as planned.

He had a dream of becoming a doctor and following in the footsteps of his father and grandfather. They were both radiologists and my friend wanted to study in Bloemfontein just as his dad and grandfather did.

Medicine was in his blood. In matric he applied to study medicine, but was not accepted. He decided to get into the program no matter what the cost. He started studying BSc. Biological Sciences at the University of Pretoria. He applied for medicine again after 6 months. He was driven and determined. Nothing could stand in his way. Soon his determination was tested.

In February that same year, at the age of 18, he was diagnosed with prostate cancer. Just like any other cancer it made his life come to a complete stand still. He couldn't continue with his studies and started with treatment right away. He lost the opportunity to study medicine that year and could only apply for the following year. He was devastated. However, his faith was strong and he changed his attitude about the situation. He embraced the year and all its opportunities and made the best of it. Spiritually he grew immensely and I know his faith deepened.

We were friends in school but somehow lost contact. I heard about his circumstances and we met for coffee. We understood each other's situations and frustrations. We were both delayed in our dreams and we encouraged one another to carry on reminding ourselves that it was only a season and that it too shall pass. Somehow we ended up fishing together and shared lists of must-read books.

He still had the dream of becoming a doctor and applied again at all the universities across the country. Determined and patiently, he waited for the response. I can still remember the morning he called me with the news: He got accepted to study medicine at the University of the Free State, his initial preference.

God knew his dream and He was faithful to my friend as He always is. God knew the right timing and the right place. My friend learned many valuable lessons through his journey with cancer which would make him an even better doctor. When I think about his story, it always gives me hope. We only see our situations and limitations, but God sees the whole picture and plans our path with a purpose. He is still in control. All things come together for good to those who love Him.

November came sooner than expected and I was off to New Zealand. I was excited to see my friend and visit a beautiful country. God blessed me by letting me go. He had a purpose with the trip.

I knew my friend since 2009 and I always had great respect for him and his faith. As I got to know him I always admired how his faith was intertwined with everything he talked about and all that he did. It came naturally and in such a real way – with no pretension.

I grew up attending church and always believed in God and His abilities. It is a miracle that I was healed from cancer twice, and I couldn't deny His part in my healing. I loved reading my Bible and listening to worship music, but it did not come naturally. It was as if my faith was in a box. Only when I had the time I would open up my box of faith and spend time talking to God or reading His Word. It was always one way - me speaking to God. I never had the same personal relationship with Jesus as my friend had.

One day we were walking on the beach and started a conversation about religion and faith. I tried to explain to him that I longed to have the same faith that he had. I asked him to explain what he did for faith to become part of his everyday life, decisions and actions. He couldn't identify anything which he did to lead him where he was in his faith. I then realised that it came from inside. He had a sense of peace in his heart and in his life. I knew it was something that I missed, something more that I longed for.

And so my "real" faith journey started. I knew that there was something more that I longed for and I was hungry for it. As a child I spoke to my Sunday school teacher about heaven. I listened and agreed with the sermons about eternal life. It still was not something I felt worthy of. I couldn't boldly declare that I knew I would go to heaven if I died that day. I always felt that good deeds and a life without sin would be my ticket to heaven.

I longed that my faith was strong enough to believe that God would listen and answer my prayers. I wanted to have faith and trust in His plans and promises for my life. I wanted my faith to follow His ways and have peace that He knows best. I realised that I never really understood the Gospel of Christ. I sought answers in Christian books and attended more church services to find directions.

There was nothing I could do to bring me the peace and faith that I longed for. I concentrated too much on "faith" itself and looked passed the Source of faith. It was only Jesus and a relationship with Him that could save me and give me what I longed for. I was determined to seek Jesus and find faith in Him.

# faith like a mustard seed

The Kingdom of Heaven is like a mustard seed planted in a field. It is the smallest of all the seeds, but it becomes the largest of garden plants; it grows into a tree, and the birds come and make nests in its branches
Matthew 13:31-32 (NLT)

So Jesus said to them, "Because of your unbelief; for assuredly, I say to you, if you have faith as a mustard seed, you will say to this mountain, 'Move from here to there,' and it will move; and nothing will be impossible for you.
Matthew 17:20 (NKJV)

THE PHYSICAL FACTS:
- Average size of a mustard seed is 1-2 millimeters.
- Certain plants can grow up to 3-5 meters high and wide.

THE SPIRITUAL SIGNIFICANCE:
- The Church of Christ (kingdom of heaven) arose from humble beginnings and so too can our church today initially start small.
- When we testify and spread the gospel of Christ, the Church can spread and accomplish the destiny of its creation.
- Although it starts small, the Church of Christ under God's blessings, authority and power, can grow and will fulfill its purpose to prepare for the coming of our Savior.

CHAPTER 13

*amazing grace*

The new year started and I was refreshed and ready for a new challenge. I wasn't accepted to study medicine, but I enrolled for the BSc. Biological Sciences program at the University of Pretoria. I was excited to start and I put all my hopes into getting accepted for medicine after six months.

As my first year started I was on a roll. My year of rest and restoration was long forgotten. I was in res and had a great time meeting new friends and attending social events. It was all fun and games, but I was still determined to find what I was longing for in my spiritual life. On Sundays, my friends and I would attend different churches near the university. One Sunday I was looking for a lift because my car was at the garage to be serviced. I was usually the taxi so I called a friend to return the favour.

We went to a church where I had not been before. It was of a charismatic nature and I didn't know what to expect. I grew up in a conservative Dutch Reformed Church. I was not used to the ways of charismatic churches. However, when the service started, I knew I was home. The praise and worship were on fire and I experienced the tangible presence of the Holy Spirit.

The pastor spoke about salvation and having the assurance of eternal life. He called on those who wanted to accept Jesus as their Saviour and opened their hearts and lives for a personal relationship with God. I immediately knew that the call was meant for me. On 9 June 2013 I became a born-again Christian. I gave my heart to Jesus and came to salvation – it was the best day of my life. I found what I so desperately sought and longed for. Not in the church, but in meeting my personal Saviour and accepting Him as my Lord.

Things did not change instantly. The more I became involved the more I learned and recognised God's revelations in my life. Through His love for me, I acquainted myself with His character. I was eager to spend time in His Presence and to study His Word. Soon my relationship with Jesus became more intimate and personal. I joined a life group and was immediately connected to other believers for fellowship that taught me more about the walk with God.

I have always served God according to my own time and convenience, but this time I knew I needed to surrender and follow where He leads me. I wanted to be involved and learn as much as possible so I joined the Kids' Ministry. There I learned what it meant to submit to authority and serve those around you. I experienced the blessing of serving and the joy that comes from it. I knew that God had led me to a church that I could call home. There I could know Him and grow in Him.

→»··«←

My health was excellent! I was still on monthly maintenance chemo treatment to keep everything under control and prevent a relapse. Sometimes it felt as if the devil attacked me and caused fear and doubt. I believed that God had twice healed me from cancer but at times I still became paranoid and regarded any symptom as a sign of a relapse. Fortunately I had great leaders and support from the church which helped me search for God's Word for reassurance and hope. As soon as I reminded myself that God loves me the fear was gone. God is love and love casts out ALL fear!

Living out my newly found faith I often reflected on my past. I saw and remembered God's faithful hand along the way. He was present daily although I did not know Him the way I know Him now. His Grace was upon me. Now I realise that the challenges made me stronger and built my character for my future. It gave me hope.

Finally I understood that I would not be good enough to work my way into heaven. According to Ephesians 2:8-10, salvation is a gift from God, not earned, but can only be accomplished through faith. This means that you have to believe in your heart and confess with your mouth to the death, burial, and resurrection of Jesus Christ as payment for your sins. After I understood these truths and made them my own I knew that I need not work for my salvation nor could I lose it. It is a pure gift from God! I was relieved that I am forgiven and that I have the Holy Spirit living within me. I could be all that I needed to be – all that God created me to be. I was saved through His Grace which is enough for me. Previously it had always been about me and what I wanted to do and become, but after I surrendered my life completely it became His Story and my testimony.

# grace like a wave

Act on God's command as He calls you to "Come". Give the leap of faith and walk your life with Him.
He will make you walk on water.

But me he caught - reached all the way from the sky to sea; he pulled me out of that ocean of hate, that enemy chaos, the void in which I was drowning.I stood there saved - surprised to be loved!"
Psalm 16-19 (MSG)

his grace is like the ocean's waves, there will always be another one.

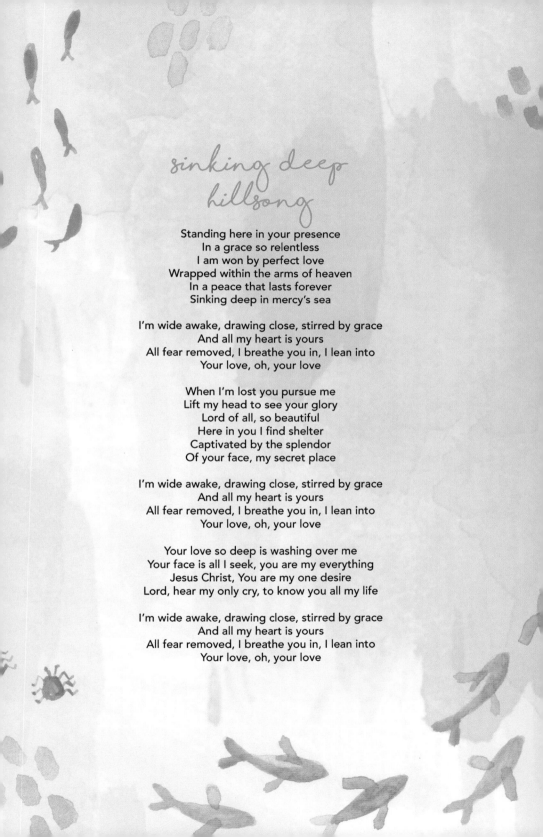

# sinking deep
## hillsong

Standing here in your presence
In a grace so relentless
I am won by perfect love
Wrapped within the arms of heaven
In a peace that lasts forever
Sinking deep in mercy's sea

I'm wide awake, drawing close, stirred by grace
And all my heart is yours
All fear removed, I breathe you in, I lean into
Your love, oh, your love

When I'm lost you pursue me
Lift my head to see your glory
Lord of all, so beautiful
Here in you I find shelter
Captivated by the splendor
Of your face, my secret place

I'm wide awake, drawing close, stirred by grace
And all my heart is yours
All fear removed, I breathe you in, I lean into
Your love, oh, your love

Your love so deep is washing over me
Your face is all I seek, you are my everything
Jesus Christ, You are my one desire
Lord, hear my only cry, to know you all my life

I'm wide awake, drawing close, stirred by grace
And all my heart is yours
All fear removed, I breathe you in, I lean into
Your love, oh, your love

# the great unknown

My years as a student were very blessed. As previously mentioned, I was not accepted to study medicine but felt that I needed a change. After countless prayers and counselling, I changed to BSc. Human Genetics. The course was very interesting but also challenging. I often doubted whether I would be able to complete it. I had a great passion for biological science and human genetics fascinated me, but I still wasn't sure that I wanted to pursue a career in that field.

After blood, sweat and tears, I graduated! My friends knew what a miracle that had been. When I had to decide what to do next I was clueless. Although I was passionate about the field of genetics the opportunities were scarce and unfamiliar. My parents relocated to Kleinmond in the Western Cape and suggested that I relocate with them and use the next year to make a proper decision about my future. It would be another step into the unknown.

I found the transition challenging. The transition from university to the work place proved to be quite daunting. There were many factors to take into consideration and I felt overwhelmed.  I gained knowledge at university, but I realised that I lacked the wisdom to make a life-changing decision. Only through prayer, faith and God's divine intervention did I find the perfect job for that season.

Throughout my course I was introduced to and interested in movement education for children. It sounded like something I would enjoy while I decided what I wanted to do for the rest of my life. I sent out various application emails and was eventually accepted by a woman from Monkeynastix in Hermanus.

God answered my prayers. I was walking into the unknown. But I was excited for the new adventure in a completely new season of my life.

The first step was to attend the instructor course in a small town in the Overberg region. The course started with a devotional address. The theme was about how God would always go before you in any situation and meet you in the unknown. He would straighten your path and secure and guide your every step regardless of how uncertain the future. He has it all planned and is in control. I had so much peace. I didn't know what to expect from the year ahead and from my new environment and people I would meet. I knew, however, that God was with me and that He would be with me every step of the way. I didn't know it at the time, but that message was applicable to the rest of my year.

→»··«←

The year started off with a bang. I quickly had to adapt and find my way around town. I joined a congregation and it gave me a place to worship and serve in God's Kingdom. I met many special people and had great leaders to mentor me. I joined the music ministry and found such joy in sharing my passion for singing and worshiping God.

Everything was going well. I thoroughly enjoyed working with the children and it gave me joy to be able to impart knowledge to them.

I was transferred to a new haematologist in Cape Town. My health was excellent. The doctor approved my maintenance treatment plan and suggested that we continue as before.

I was, however not content during that time. I am a goal-driven and ambitious person and it felt like I was not fulfilling my purpose yet. God's promises tested my faith, but He gave me peace about the future. Although nothing was in vain and even though it felt as if my future was unknown, God still had a plan for me.

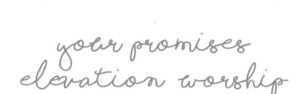

# your promises
## elevation worship

When the weight of the world begins to fall
On the Name of Jesus I will call
For I know my God is in control
and His purpose is unshakable

Doesn't matter what I feel
Doesn't matter what I see
My hope will always be
In Your promises to me
Now I'm casting out all fear
For Your love has set me free
My hope will always be
In Your promises to me

As I walk into the days to come
I will not forget what You have done
For you have supplied my every need
And Your presence is enough for me

You will always be more than enough for me
You will always be more than enough for me
Nothing's gonna stop the plans You've made
Nothing's gonna take Your love away
You will always be more than enough for me

Doesn't matter what I feel
Doesn't matter what I see
My hope will always be
In Your promises to me
Now I'm casting out all fear
For Your love has set me free
My hope will always be
In Your promises to me

# new season

On the 12th of March 2016 our town had its CANSA Relay for Life. It is a fundraising event for cancer survivors and patients. My mother survived her own battle with breast cancer so we were invited to do a fun walk throughout the night in awareness of cancer and pay tribute to those who lost the battle. As we took part I was once again reminded of my 10-year journey with cancer. I was thankful to reflect on how God had carried me through everything, healed me twice and made me stronger.

Three days later on the 15th of March, I received a call from my haematologist in connection with a possible bone marrow transplant. He had reconsidered my treatment plan and felt that it was necessary to proceed with the transplant to ensure a cancer-free future. We had considered the transplant in the past, but this call and the news he shared was completely unexpected.

The next morning my parents and I drove to Cape Town. I did not know what to expect. My emotions were similar to those I experienced on the day I received my first diagnosis. I knew that my life could change in an instant.

We had a formal meeting with the doctor. He questioned us about my previous treatment. He wanted to know why a bone marrow transplant had not been done. I explained to him that it was cancelled due to the search for a suitable donor and my infection.

He advised us that a transplant was the only way to prevent a future relapse. He explained that I couldn't continue with my current maintenance treatment plan indefinitely, since it has adverse side effects. He was very clear that I could not stop my treatment either because the risk for another relapse was greater.

It was a difficult decision to make. I was healthy at that time and it was hard to imagine that I was still at risk for a relapse without the transplant. We raised our concerns about the risks involved with the transplant. The doctor assured us that the treatment and technology had since advanced and developed in such a way that there were fewer risks involved and better success in managing them. At first I was in total shock. I felt that my life would once again have to come to a standstill. I would have had to sacrifice another year of my future to deal with the treatment, transplant, and recovery. Fortunately time was not of the essence and I requested that the transplant be scheduled for the following year. I wanted to finish the job I had started and prepare for the process. Even though it seemed frightening and uncertain I knew that God was guiding me.

When the shock passed I realised a few amazing things. God had planned it all along. I was not to have the transplant in 2011. Now was the right time to go through with it. Back then, my parents had started planning on me having the transplant in Cape Town. It would have disrupted our lives too much. I was in the perfect place and time where God had placed me for the transplant. I was close to the hospital and the environment was ideal for recovery after a transplant – with fresh air and the sea to enjoy.

I also learned that I miraculously ended up at the doctor I was initially intended to go to. The fact that the timing, setting and the technicalities were all in my favour made me realise that God is Sovereign! He planned it all along in the most exquisite detail. His will prevailed - that gave me peace.

→»··«←

I had a wonderful year and embraced every moment. I was regularly reminded about the season that lay ahead. I stilled my concerns by spending time in God's presence and reminded myself that He started this process and would lead it to a successful completion. I decided to be as healthy and strong as I possibly could. I desperately wanted the transplant to be successful and have a full recovery afterwards.

I followed a healthy diet and kept myself fit whilst enjoying my work with the children and spending valuable time with friends and family. Whenever my thoughts drifted towards sadness about the time I would have to sacrifice and be in isolation, I motivated myself to make the best of every moment.

By the end of the year I had a wonderful vacation with some friends, travelled to the family for Christmas and tried to spend as much time with as many people as possible since I would not have the opportunity for a while. I was blessed in abundance by God with all the special memories that I made with the people closest and dearest to me.

A new season awaited me. I knew that it would require of me to fight again, but I also knew that God would be with me every step of the way. It felt as if I was preparing for a time of drought – spiritual drought. I spiritually gathered enough strength to carry me through the season that lay ahead. I didn't know what the new season would have in store for me. All I knew was that I should still my heart, be still and remember Who is fighting for me.

# seasons change
# hillsong worship

Like the frost on a rose
Winter comes for us all
Oh how nature acquaints us
With the nature of patience
Like a seed in the snow
I've been buried to grow
For Your promise is loyal
From seed to sequoia

I know
Though the winter is long even richer
The harvest it brings
Though my waiting prolongs even greater
Your promise for me like a seed
I believe that my season will come

Lord I think of Your love
Like the low winter sun
And as I gaze I am blinded
In the light of Your brightness
And like a fire to the snow
I'm renewed in Your warmth
Melt the ice of this wild soul
Till the barren is beautiful

I can see the promise
I can see the future
You're the God of seasons
And I'm just in the winter
If all I know of harvest
Is that it's worth my patience
Then if You're not done working
God I'm not done waiting
You can see my promise

Even in the winter
Cause You're the God of greatness
Even in a manger
For all I know of seasons
Is that You take Your time
You could have saved us in a second
Instead You sent a child

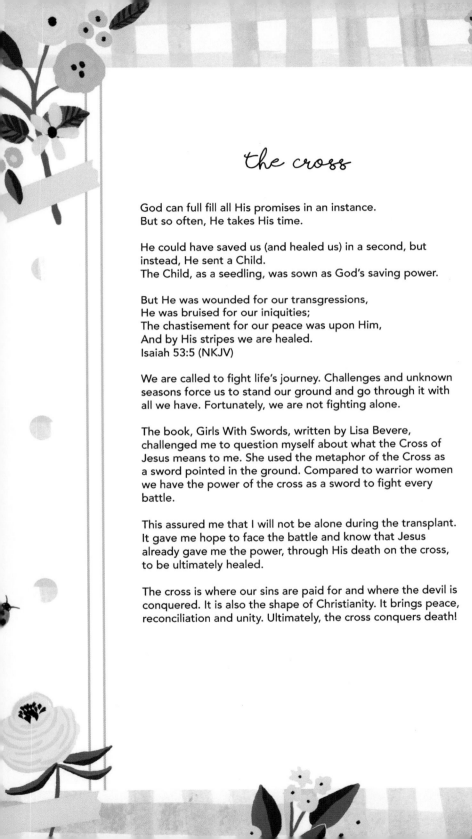

# the cross

God can full fill all His promises in an instance.
But so often, He takes His time.

He could have saved us (and healed us) in a second, but
instead, He sent a Child.
The Child, as a seedling, was sown as God's saving power.

But He was wounded for our transgressions,
He was bruised for our iniquities;
The chastisement for our peace was upon Him,
And by His stripes we are healed.
Isaiah 53:5 (NKJV)

We are called to fight life's journey. Challenges and unknown
seasons force us to stand our ground and go through it with
all we have. Fortunately, we are not fighting alone.

The book, Girls With Swords, written by Lisa Bevere,
challenged me to question myself about what the Cross of
Jesus means to me. She used the metaphor of the Cross as
a sword pointed in the ground. Compared to warrior women
we have the power of the cross as a sword to fight every
battle.

This assured me that I will not be alone during the transplant.
It gave me hope to face the battle and know that Jesus
already gave me the power, through His death on the cross,
to be ultimately healed.

The cross is where our sins are paid for and where the devil is
conquered. It is also the shape of Christianity. It brings peace,
reconciliation and unity. Ultimately, the cross conquers death!

WHAT DOES THE CROSS
MEAN TO YOU?

forgiveness

healing

power

salvation

reconciliation

protection

# when the fight calls
## hillsong young + free

You've overcome this world with love
And made my fight Your own
I lift my eyes and throw fear aside
And sing out into the night

'Cause even when the world caves
Even when the fight calls
Even when the war's waged
I'll take heart
I know You are greater
Forever You are Savior
I will sing Your praise
With all that I have
With all that "I am", Lord

I'll stare down the waves
'Cause You own the tide
I still my soul and know
You wait for me
On waters wild
Where faith walks above the storm

Even when the world caves
Even when the fight calls
Even when the war's waged
I'll take heart
I know You are greater
Forever You are Savior
I will sing Your praise
With all that I have
With all that "I am", Lord

I won't let the storm weather my heart
Won't let the darkness beat me down
Sing in the night my hope alive in You
I'll walk through the fire and not be burned
Pray in the fight and watch it turn
Jesus tonight I give it all to You

# let the fight begin

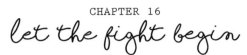

Preparing for the transplant was tough. It challenged me on physical, spiritual and emotional levels.

The first step was to determine whether we had funding for the transplant. Fortunately I was on an extensive medical aid plan that would cover it. There was, however, a significant delay in the administration of my application for funding. This tested my faith immensely. The response was delayed for about 6 months which compromised the search for a donor too. During that time I was frustrated but tried to keep reminding myself that all is in God's hands. There must be a reason for this delay.

Finally I got the approval for funding and the search for a donor began. We knew from the previous tests that there were no possible donors in South Africa. A search commenced on the international Stem Cell Registry Database. There are over 31 million potential donors on the database that had to be matched with my DNA. They use genetic testing to find the most suitable genetic match for your cell's tissue type. After a lengthy search a match was found and I was contacted with the good news. It was a 24-year old German girl from Poland. I was in awe of the outcome and thankful as I had heard of multiple cancer patients who were in desperate need and search for a donor.

As further preparation I had to study the process of the transplant and the possible side effects. One of the long-term side effects can be infertility. This is caused by the high dosage of chemotherapy and targeted drugs used to break down the immune system to prevent rejection after the transplant. I dreamt of becoming a mother one day and decided to store my eggs as a precaution. It was a frightening process, but I am thankful that I had the opportunity to do whatever I could to ensure a future family.

Throughout the rest of the year, I experienced many emotions. There were fear, anxiety, sadness and loneliness. I realised that I was going to lose my hair again and this time it was harder for me. It didn't bother me as much previously, but this time I was a young woman and it frightened me to think that I was going to be bald again. God comforted me throughout. He showed me to set my eyes on the future and not focus on the temporary. It was all for my greater good and helped me to endure the present.

On the 17th of February 2017 the central line was inserted into my chest. It would be utilised during the treatment and afterwards to administer medication, donor cells and to draw blood. All went well with the procedure and I spent the weekend at home.

That concluded my preparation. I was ready for the transplant. The transplant which was supposed to happen six years ago was finally about to take place. It was part of the promise for the greater future that God had planned for me.

# jireh
# elevation worship
# + maverick city

I'll never be more loved than I am right now
Wasn't holding You up
So there's nothing I can do to let You down
It doesn't take a trophy to make You proud
I'll never be more loved than I am right now

Going through a storm but I won't go down
I hear Your voice
Carried in the rhythm of the wind to call me out
You would cross an ocean so I wouldn't drown
You've never been closer than You are right now

You are Jireh, You are enough
And I will be content in every circumstance
You are Jireh, You are enough

Forever enough
Always enough
More than enough

If He dresses the lilies with beauty and splendor
How much more will He clothe you?
If He watched over every sparrow
How much more does He love you?

You are Jireh, You are enough

CHAPTER 17

## faithful father

The following Thursday morning, the 23rd of February, my mom and I made the final trip to Constantiaberg Medi-Clinic for the transplant. I was stressed and we both were quiet during the drive. When we arrived I settled into my new room where I would be for the next few weeks.

The Bone Marrow Transplant Centre has a dedicated isolation facility for patients undergoing a stem cell transplant. There are only a few rooms that are strictly controlled. The overall purpose is to keep the patients in a germ-free environment while their blood cell counts are low.

I had my own room with a view on the hospital's main entrance. It kept me entertained to see people coming and going. As a constant reminder of my faith, I took posters with scriptures to put on the wall. I did not know whether I would be in the mood to do anything so I packed a variety of things to keep me busy with. They even provided me with a stationary bicycle as they encouraged me to keep on exercising for my physical and mental health.

Friends and family could visit me in the transplant unit. However, there were strict protocols for them to follow. At the entrance of the unit there was a room where they had to change into protective clothing and put all their belongings in lockers. It was ultimately to prevent any germs from entering the unit.

I received chemotherapy for the next six days with another drug that was made out of horse enzymes. That was meant to break down any remaining cells that the chemotherapy didn't. Initially I didn't experience any side effects from the chemotherapy but the other drug affected me as it was known to cause a reaction. I was sleepy from the pre-medication and the drug itself made me nauseous. Fortunately that came to an end. On the sixth day, the day before the transplant, I had a rest day.

As I woke on the day of the transplant I was very sick. I was nauseous and constantly vomited. I had diarrhoea too. I felt like a wreck. The nurses told me that it was caused by underlying stress and my anxiousness about the transplant. My mom, dad, sister, brother-in-law, grandmother, dearest friend - Frances and the pastor came to join the ceremony before the transplant. I was given pre-medication that made me quite sleepy, but I tried to follow as best I could.

The procedure of the transplant was explained to us. We lit a candle. My pastor shared a message of hope and prayed before the donor stem cells were administered. Thereafter, everything was a blur. The line was connected and everybody left the room. I was asleep for the rest of the day. I awoke late in the afternoon. All felt like a dream to me but I was certain that my hope for a healthy future was restored.

→»··«←

I had a fair idea of what the transplant process would entail and I prepared myself accordingly. I knew that I was going to experience bad times, but it hit me harder than I expected. A few weeks prior to the transplant, we had a message at church about Daniel. The moral of the message was that life is full of fires and that all of us would one day face a fire or two. We had to remember that God would sometimes deliver us from the fire, but at other times He will deliver us through the fire. At times we had to go through the fire to refine us into the shape that God intended us to be for the future He had planned for us. In those tough days, I realised that I was not going to be delivered from this time in the hospital and from the side effects that I will have to endure, but that God will safely guide and protect me through it all. Some days were more challenging than others, but luckily I had that promise to hold onto. He is a faithful Father!

I can honestly say that I only had minor side effects and reactions to the transplant. I was nauseous and had a few days of diarrhoea. One day my temperature spiked which caused rigours that made me shake and shiver extensively. I was treated and it soon passed. My appetite decreased due to the nausea so a feeding tube was inserted to ensure that my body received sufficient nutrition to recover strongly.

As the days passed, I reflected and felt that I was getting better and stronger. I was discharged on the 17th of March, my 23rd day in hospital – only 15 days post-transplant. Everyone was in awe at how well I had recovered and how strong I was when I walked out of the Bone Marrow Transplant Unit. It felt terrific to walk outside and feel the sun on my skin again and see some people around me. God was so good and faithful during the whole transplant process. I was extremely thankful for my successful treatment and recovery.

# final chapter

The transplant had been done and I was in the recovery phase. I was on a strict low-microbial diet and needed to check myself regularly for any symptoms of an infection or rejection. I also underwent weekly treatment for a period of twelve weeks. During that period I kept myself busy with crafts and projects. I felt stronger day by day. I went for daily walks along Beach road and continued writing this book. I sometimes had to remind myself not to be too anxious about moving on with my life. I had to be content and embrace the season of rest that I was in.

After three months of self-isolation I had to avoid becoming depressed. I was lonely and uncertain about the future. I spent a lot of time crying out to God and asking Him for answers. I desperately wanted to follow His will – but I didn't know what it was. I was impatient and was ready to get on with my life. I didn't know which direction to follow. Whenever I thought I had enough information for a plan I came across a limitation that kept me from going forward. At times I was negative, but refrained from voicing my frustrations and fears because I knew it wouldn't help. I tried to stay positive and speak life over my future. It forced me to utter all my worries and frustrations to God. He was my great Counsellor throughout that time. Today I am thankful because it made me grow and be more intimate in my relationship with Him.

One night I was extremely frustrated. I kept asking Him for directions and answers, but He didn't respond. Bible in hand, I prayed to Him again asking for ANY answers and guidance. I was determined to read the Bible for as long as necessary and was not about to stop until I found something that I could hold onto – ANYTHING! As I finished my prayer Proverbs 3 immediately came to mind. I was disappointed at first. I knew the chapter and thought that I would not find the revelation I was looking for. Oh, but God knew exactly what I needed to hear. When I eagerly started reading, I realised that verses five and six were the answer! I had all I needed! How could I have forgotten?

*Trust God from the bottom of your heart;*
*don't try to figure out everything on your own.*
*Listen for God's voice in everything you do, everywhere you*
*go; He's the one who will keep you on track.*
Proverbs 3:5-6 (MSG)

God was saying to me, "Trust, be still and wait on Me." I then knew that I needed to be patient. He didn't forget about me. I came to the realisation that He would complete the work He started in me. He had it all planned and I just needed to trust and acknowledge Him. He would show me the way as well as what to do. He was and still is in control!

I truly believe that this was the final chapter of my season with cancer. I am healed and given new life through Jesus Christ. The chapter of cancer had been concluded with the transplant, but not of my life. God has given me a new and abundant life through His Grace! I don't know what the future holds in store, but I know that it will be good and more than I could ever dream of. The same applies to us all. God wants us to live the generous life which Jesus came to give us. We only need to invite Him into our lives to receive it.

# peace be still
# the belonging co.

I don't want to be afraid
Every time I face the waves
I don't want to be afraid

I don't want to fear the storm
Just because I hear it roar
I don't want to fear the storm

Peace be still
Say the word and I will
Set my feet upon the sea
Till I'm dancing in the deep
Peace be still
You are here so it is well
Even when my eyes can't see
I will trust the voice that speaks

Peace
Peace over me

# CHAPTER 19

# the unexpected season

I was convinced that I had written the final chapter of my long journey. I was healed from cancer and ready to move on. Thankfully, I recovered well after the transplant and was more than prepared to live my life to the full.

I was ready to pursue my future, but found myself at crossroads. I had to decide what direction I wanted to take professionally but was not sure. My only option with my Bachelor of Sciences degree seemed to be in education. I regarded it as a temporary option as I still had to pursue the "bigger dream". I was convinced that it was something more significant than teaching. I idolised a career in medicine and believed that it was the only way I can full fill the purpose of my life. Meanwhile, God knew better and had greater plans.

I was fortunate enough to land a teaching position at a school in Cape Town. Although it happened fast I was excited to face the new challenge. I relocated and immediately started at the school. Man, oh man, was I surprised! It was the best thing that could ever have happened to me.

I realised that it was my true calling to be a teacher. I was excited to go to school every day. It is so rewarding to be part of every child's life and to impart knowledge. I repented for regarding a career in education as inferior. I came to the realisation of the critical role it plays in society.

Adapting to a new career and studying part-time for a Post Graduate Certificate in Education was a challenge. After being isolated for so long I had to find my feet again and settle into the new community. Luckily, I joined a congregation where I found an incredible support system.

Things were starting to settle in. It was not something that I was used to. I had been functioning in survival mode for the longest time. I had to cope with challenges and changes at hand. I became skilled to operate in crisis mode, but the everyday balanced routine type of life was one I found hard to manage. It was then that the feelings that I had suppressed from my past surfaced.

In the past I had to be strong and fight every battle with cancer and other challenges. With God's help I was able to do it. I had, however, never learnt to deal with the emotions that came with the trauma. I was under the false impression that if I talk about my struggles I would be regarded as weak and without faith. I became used to suppressing my feelings and they bottled up inside of me until there was no more space.

This caused an unexpected season in my life which hit me the hardest. My faith was challenged to the limit. I was at the lowest emotional point in my life.

We all react differently to trauma and the effect needs to be dealt with otherwise, it manifests in other ways. In my case the repeated trauma and the fact that I didn't work through it properly, caused my hormone levels to be suppressed. Without being aware of it I developed depression, anxiety and obsessiveness.

I reached an all time low because of the depression. It felt like I was in a dark hole and I wasn't strong enough to get out. The loneliness was overwhelming because I didn't know who to talk to. I desperately needed help, but it felt like my prayers were not being answered. I couldn't understand why God didn't deliver me from the bondage at that moment. I repented and prayed much, but I kept falling into my old ways. I surrendered and asked God to take control, but it didn't improve. I felt ashamed because I thought my faith was not strong enough. I was desperate to be freed from it all and I reached a point where I knew I needed help.

Even though I thought God wasn't hearing me, I had this conviction that through it all God is still God. He would remain faithful in this situation. His miracles from my past kept me hoping for ultimate healing.

Thankfully I had a loving friend who directed me to the right people. I reached out and received the help I needed. It was the best I could do. It took courage and boldness to step out of my comfort zone but I knew God was behind it all.

I know now that He is using my story for His glory.

I learned that it is okay not to be okay. We are human and challenging times make us more aware of our dependency on God. Through His strength we will be okay again. Depression is something that the enemy uses to try and knock us down but in God we have the victory to overcome it. God uses people to work in our lives and that is not a sign of weak faith to reach out for help. It is a sign of courage to fight for the better life God wants you to live. He doesn't want you to suffer – He wants you to be an overcomer.

There may come a time when you feel alone or depressed. Reach out to those around you. Don't isolate yourself. Get the help that you need – it is worth it! God loves you dearly and has a greater plan for you – plans of hope and a future. It is time for you to believe it and pursue the life He wants you to have. Use the Maker as your mirror to see your potential. Believe the things He says about you and find Hope in Him and His promises for you.

# CHAPTER 20

# hope in my heart

This is my story for now. God has been so faithful during my life and surprised me with a life that is more than I could ever have dreamed of or ask for. I believe this is only the start of what God has planned for my life. Every season brings a new chapter and a new powerful testimony of His goodness and faithfulness. I am excited about the rest of my life.

Whenever I get the opportunity to share my story and encourage someone else who is going through something similar I feel as if it completes the purpose of my journey.

At the moment I am trying to live content in the season that I find myself in. I am still teaching and enjoying every moment of it. The career has many challenges but it also offers many opportunities to grow professionally and personally. My passion for children motivates me to make a difference and bring hope into the lives of others.

I am open-minded about the future. Hope is what carried me, healed me and brought me to where I am today. That is why I have Hope for my future. Hope for a life partner and for a family to love. Hope for my loved ones and for Christ to be known by all.

This is just a part of my story and I look forward to see how the rest unfolds.

But for now, I am going to trust Him, acknowledge Him in all I do and follow wherever He directs my steps. He knows the plans He has for me and it is good and peaceful. I will always have Hope in my heart.

The rest is still unwritten...

*hope begins with you!*

DKMS is an international charity dedicated to fight against blood cancer and blood disorders. They fight blood diseases like leukaemia through the recruitment of stem cell donors and maintaining a registry of potential donors committed to helping anyone in need of a live-saving stem cell transplant. They raise funds to cover the cost of education and awareness about the need for and the process to become a blood stem cell donor as well as to cover the cost of the HLA tissue-typing test involved in the recruitment of donors.

DKMS also maintains a patient support fund to assist patients who are unable to afford costs associated with getting to transplant as well as being actively involved in creating a platform for support structures to assist patients, families and communities.

Together we can fight life-threatening blood diseases. Be somebody's hope for live by registering to be a stem cell donor, donating money or volunteering.

For more information and contact details visit their web page
www.dkms.org

**DKMS** x
WE DELETE BLOOD CANCER